P9-CAO-356

Fort McHenry

Charles W. Maynard

The Rosen Publishing Group's
PowerKids Press™
New York

In memory of Charles, Velma, Relland, Erma, Martha, Sheila, Lynn, and those who went on before

Published in 2002 by The Rosen Publishing Group, Inc.
29 East 21st Street, New York, NY 10010

First Edition

Book Design: Michael Caroleo

Project Editor: Kathy Campbell

Photo Credits: p. 4 © Richard T. Nowitz/CORBIS; p. 7 (Fort McHenry) © Paul A. Souders/CORBIS; pp. 7 (diagram), 15, 16 (statue), 19, 20 © Janice Maynard; p. 8 © SuperStock; p. 11 (all) © North Wind Pictures; p. 12 (cannons) © Index Stock, (flag) © The Smithsonian Institution; p. 16 (fort) © Charles E. Rotkin/CORBIS.

Maynard, Charles W. (Charles William), 1955-
Fort McHenry / Charles W. Maynard.
p. cm. — (Famous forts throughout American history)
Includes index.
ISBN 0-8239-5838-8 (lib. bdg.)
1. Fort McHenry (Baltimore, Md.)—Juvenile literature. 2. Fort McHenry National Monument and Historic Shrine (Baltimore, Md.)—Juvenile literature. 3. Baltimore (Md.)—Buildings, structures, etc.—Juvenile literature. 4. Baltimore (Md.)—History, Military—Juvenile literature.
[1. Fort McHenry (Baltimore, Md.) 2. United States—History—War of 1812.] I. Title.
E356.B2 M39 2002
975.2'6-dc21

00-012483

Manufactured in the United States of America

Contents

Top: *A map shows the location of Baltimore and Whetstone Point. The first fort on the point was called Fort Whetstone.* Bottom: *Today Fort McHenry, a star-shaped fort, is only about 3 miles (4.8 km) from the center of Baltimore.*

Baltimore and Fort Whetstone

By the time of the **American Revolution** (1775–1783), Baltimore, Maryland, was an important and growing town. Baltimore's value came from its location as a seaport, where ships docked to load or unload cargo.

During the Revolution, the people of Baltimore wanted to guard their harbor from British attacks. The best place for a fort to defend Baltimore was on Whetstone Point at the end of a 1-mile-long (1.6 km-long) **peninsula** 2 miles (3.2 km) south of the city. The Patapsco River flowed on both sides of Whetstone Point.

Local patriots built a star-shaped fort, Fort Whetstone, on the point to shoot at any British ships that might sail into the port. The British did not attack the fort during the Revolution, so the patriots there did not fire any shots. When the war ended, the patriots deserted the fort.

Building Fort McHenry

In 1793, Great Britain and France began to fight each other in a war. People in the United States feared that the fighting would come to America, and so they began to prepare for war. The citizens of Maryland asked the government to build a fort to protect the city's harbor. Workmen, under the direction of French engineer Jean Foncin, built a star-shaped, brick fort with five **bastions**. This project lasted from 1798 to 1802. Foncin improved on plans drawn by John Jacob Ulrich Rivardi and Louis De Tousard, two Frenchmen who designed forts for the young United States. A brick **parapet** in the shape of a five-pointed star surrounded **barracks** and a **powder magazine**. A triangle-shaped **ravelin** protected the **sally port** to the fort. A dry ditch to the north and a row of **cannons** to the south gave added support to the fort. It was named Fort McHenry, for James McHenry, who had fought in the Revolution.

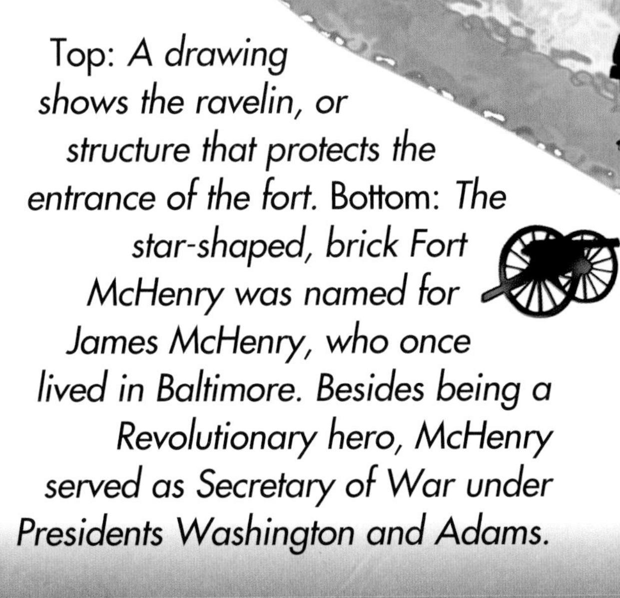

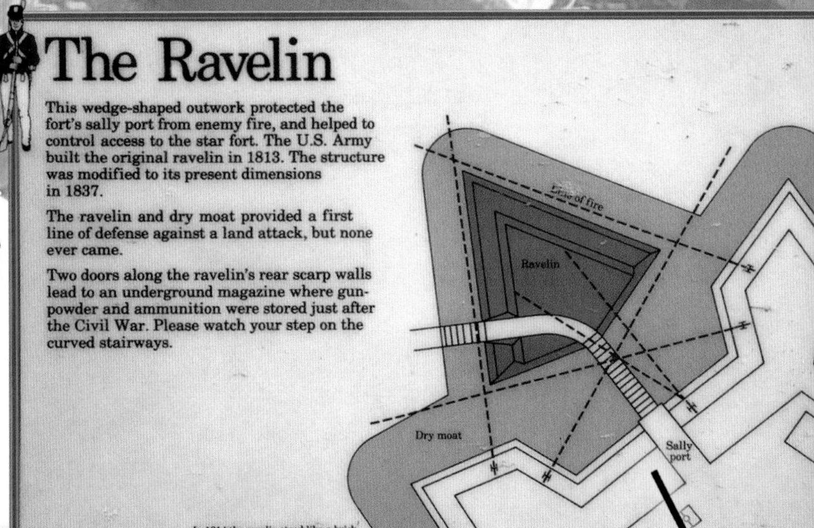

Top: *A drawing shows the ravelin, or structure that protects the entrance of the fort.* Bottom: *The star-shaped, brick Fort McHenry was named for James McHenry, who once lived in Baltimore. Besides being a Revolutionary hero, McHenry served as Secretary of War under Presidents Washington and Adams.*

On September 13 and 14, in 1814, the British bombarded Fort McHenry for 25 hours nonstop. It is believed that the British fired from 1,500 to 1,800 shells at the fort, with nearly 400 of these falling inside it.

Battle for Baltimore

The United States declared war on Great Britain in June 1812. In August 1814, the British sailed to America. The British marched to Washington, D.C., on August 24, 1814, and burned the **Capitol** and other government buildings. Baltimore was their next target.

Five thousand British troops landed near Baltimore on September 12, 1814. They had to force American troops at Fort McHenry to surrender before they could capture Baltimore. The British navy sailed near Fort McHenry to **bombard** it with rockets, bombs, and cannonballs.

Major George Armistead commanded Fort McHenry's **garrison** of 1,000 soldiers. Of the 1,000 men, only 4 were killed and 24 wounded. Major Armistead refused to **surrender** the fort or to lower the U.S. flag. The British troops could not take the fort, so they left Baltimore and sailed out into the Chesapeake Bay.

"The Star-Spangled Banner"

After burning Washington, the British troops arrested Dr. William Beanes as they marched into Maryland. Although Beanes helped the wounded of both the British and the U.S. armies, the British were upset because he had some of their soldiers arrested for **looting**.

Francis Scott Key, a lawyer and a friend of Dr. Beanes's, agreed to help obtain the release of the doctor. U.S. Colonel John Skinner and Key sailed to find the British fleet that was holding Dr. Beanes. Colonel Skinner and Key bargained with British admiral Alexander Cochrane to release Dr. Beanes. The admiral agreed to the bargain but said the three men had to stay on a ship until the British had finished bombarding Fort McHenry. He did not want Key and Skinner to warn Baltimore about the British plan to attack. The men watched all night as the British shot at Fort McHenry. At daybreak, the large U.S. flag still flew over the fort!

Top Right: *The British fleet blocked Baltimore Harbor after burning Washington, D.C.* Bottom: *In 1931, Key's poem became the U.S. national anthem "The Star-Spangled Banner."*

Francis Scott Key wrote a poem about the battle and called it "The Defense of Fort McHenry."

The Star-spangled banner.

O say! can you see by the dawn's early light
What so proudly we hail'd at the twilight's last gleaming
Whose broad stripes and bright stars, through the clouds of the fight,
O'er the ramparts we watch'd were so gallantly streaming?
And the rocket's red glare – the bomb bursting in air
Gave proof through the night that our flag was still there!
O say, does that star-spangled banner yet wave
O'er the land of the free & the home of the brave? –

Major George Armistead's family gave the Fort McHenry flag to the Smithsonian Institution in 1912. The original flag can be seen in the Smithsonian's National Museum of American History in Washington, D.C.

Fort McHenry's Flag

The U.S. flag has not always had 13 stripes and 50 stars. The flag that flew over Fort McHenry during the Battle of Baltimore in 1814 had 15 stripes and 15 stars. The 15 stars and stripes represented the first 13 states plus Vermont and Kentucky. Only later, in 1818, was the design of the flag changed to have one star for each state and one stripe for each of the 13 original colonies.

Mary Pickersgill and her 13-year-old daughter, Caroline, made Fort McHenry's flags. The fort had two flags, a storm flag measuring 17 feet by 25 feet (5.2 m by 7.6 m), and a garrison flag, which measured 30 feet by 42 feet (9.1 m by 12.8 m). The large garrison flag flew over the fort after the British bombardment, although it seems that both flags were flown during the battle. Major George Armistead, the fort's commander, kept the famous flag after the battle.

These cannons of the fort overlook the harbor.

A Military Prison

After the War of 1812, the U.S. Army built the barracks and powder magazine larger to improve Fort McHenry. From 1846 to 1848, Maryland troops trained at Fort McHenry to fight in the Mexican War (1846–1848).

During the Civil War (1861–1865), Fort McHenry became a **military** prison, a hospital, and a defense post. At the start of the war, **civilians** who were friends of the **rebellious** Southern states found themselves jailed there. Confederate prisoners joined them after the fight began. More than 7,000 Confederate prisoners arrived at Fort McHenry following the Battle of Gettysburg in July 1863. During the course of the war, nearly 15,000 people served prison time at Fort McHenry.

Fort McHenry stood as a coastal defense fort with large guns after the Civil War. Only a small garrison stayed in the fort.

Fort McHenry served as a prison during the Civil War. After the Battle of Gettysburg in July 1863, almost 7,000 Confederates were brought to the fort and put behind bars. The fort even had underground cells like the one shown here.

Top: *This statue of Major George Armistead overlooks Baltimore Harbor. Armistead commanded the soldiers at the fort from 1813 to 1818.*
Bottom: *After it served as a military hospital, Fort McHenry became a national park cared for by the U.S. Army in 1925.*

An Army Hospital

The U.S. Army officially closed the fort on July 20, 1912, when the 141st Company of Coastal Artillery moved to a new location. Fort McHenry remained an active fort for more than 125 years. At the **centennial** celebration of the Battle of Baltimore in September 1914, the people of Baltimore gave a statue of Major George Armistead to honor the men who fought at Fort McHenry.

When the United States entered World War I in 1917, the army built U.S. General Hospital Number 2 on the grounds of the old fort. This hospital contained 3,000 beds in nearly 100 buildings, making it the largest military hospital in the country. Soldiers wounded in Europe recovered at Fort McHenry.

After the last patients left in 1923, the army restored the fort to the way it looked before the Civil War.

More Than a National Shrine

"The Star-Spangled Banner" became the official national anthem of the United States in 1931. The army transferred Fort McHenry and the land around it to the National Park Service in 1933. In 1939, the fort became a national **monument** and historic **shrine**, the only place in the country then or now with such a title.

In 1941, when the United States entered World War II, the old fort that had served the country since the Revolution was put into service again. The Fort McHenry U.S. Coast Guard Fire Training Station was built in 1942 around the old buildings. People trained there to fight fires on warships and to keep the country's harbors safe. After World War II, the training station buildings were torn down. In 1959 and 1960, when Alaska and Hawaii became new states, the new U.S. flags were first flown over Fort McHenry.

If any other state is added to the United States, the new flag with the added star will fly first over Fort McHenry, just as it did on July 4, 1959, when the forty-ninth star was added for Alaska and on July 4, 1960, when the fiftieth star was added for Hawaii.

Timeline

1776 Fort Whetstone is constructed.

1798-1802 Fort McHenry is constructed.

1802 Fort McHenry is completed.

1812 Congress declares war on Great Britain.

1814 On August 24, the British attack and burn Washington, D. C.

1814 From September 12 to 14, the Battle of Baltimore is fought.

1829 Changes are made to Fort McHenry.

1846-1848 Fort McHenry is used for recruiting and training troops for the Mexican War.

1861-1865 Fort McHenry houses Confederate prisoners.

1912 On July 20, the last garrison of U.S. Army troops leaves the fort.

1917-1923 Fort McHenry is used as an Army hospital.

1925 Congress proclaims Fort McHenry a national park.

1931 On March 3, "The Star-Spangled Banner" officially becomes the national anthem.

1939 Fort McHenry National Park is declared a national monument and historic shrine.

"And the Flag Was Still There..."

Even after it was no longer used to defend the harbor and the city of Baltimore, Fort McHenry continued to serve the country as a military hospital and U.S. Coast Guard training center. Now it stands as the only historic shrine in the United States, to remind all Americans of the birth of their country's anthem, "The Star-Spangled Banner."

The most noticeable feature at the fort is the large flag of 15 stars and 15 stripes that flies on a tall pole. Fort McHenry is one of only a few places in the United States where the 15 stars and stripes flag is allowed to fly. Others are at Francis Scott Key's birthplace and grave in Maryland, the Star-Spangled Banner House in Baltimore, the U.S. *Constitution* in Baltimore Harbor, and Lewis and Clark's Fort Clatsop in Oregon.

Fort McHenry remained an active fort for more than 125 years. Many of its guns and cannons are still in place to show how the fort defended Baltimore throughout the fort's history.

Fort McHenry Today

The U.S. flag still flies over Fort McHenry today at the National Park Service site near downtown Baltimore. By special proclamation of the president of the United States, the U.S. flag is flown all the time. A visitor center at the fort tells the story of Fort McHenry and the famous Battle of Baltimore. Re-enactors and **volunteers** show what life at the fort once was like.

At the fort, statues of Major George Armistead and the Greek poet Orpheus remind people of the men who fought at Fort McHenry and of Francis Scott Key's famous poem that became our national anthem.

Special celebrations are held each year on June 14, Flag Day, and in September on Defenders' Day. Guns and cannons are in place to show how the fort looked during different times in its exciting history.

Glossary

American Revolution (uh-MER–uh-ken reh-vuh-LOO-shuhn) The war American colonists fought from 1775 to 1783 to win freedom from England.
barracks (BAR-iks) Buildings where soldiers live.
bastions (BAS-chunz) Works of earth, brick, or stone that stand out from a fortified work.
bombard (bom-BARD) To attack with artillery, such as guns and cannons.
cannons (KA-nunz) Large guns with a smooth bore barrel.
Capitol (KA-pih-tol) The building where Congress meets in Washington, D.C.
centennial (sen-TEH-nee-uhl) One hundred years.
civilians (sih-VIL-yinz) People that are not in the military.
garrison (GAR-ih-sun) A group of soldiers stationed at a fort.
looting (LOOT-ing) Breaking in and stealing.
military (MIH-lih-ter-ee) Part of the government that protects the United States; the armed forces, such as the army or the navy.
monument (MAHN-yoo-ment) Something built to honor a person or an event.
parapet (PAR-uh-pet) A wall or bank used to screen troops from enemy fire.
peninsula (peh-NIN-suh-lah) Land surrounded by water on three sides and connected to the mainland by a narrow strip.
powder magazine (POW-dur MA-guh-zeen) A bombproof room for storing gun powder and explosives.
ravelin (RAV-lin) A triangular-shaped, brick and earth structure built to protect the entrance to a fort.
rebellious (rih-BEL-yus) Resisting authority.
sally port (SA-lee PORT) The entrance to a fort, with two sets of large doors.
shrine (SHRYN) A special place in honor of an important person or event.
surrender (suh-REN-der) To give up.
volunteers (vah-lun-TEERZ) Workers who offer to help and do not get paid for their work.

Index

Web Sites

To learn more about Fort McHenry, check out these Web sites:
www.bcpl.net/~etowner/
www.nps.gov/fomc/archeology/overview.html